Contents

AGES 8–9
NUMERACY

Premier

QUICK TESTS

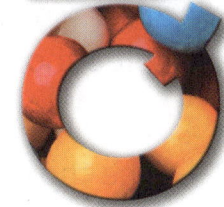

Test 1 Place value (1)

Thousands	Hundreds	Tens	Units	
4	9	5	7	= 4000 + 900 + 50 + 7

Write the missing numbers.

1. 4173 = 4000 + 100 + ☐ + 3

2. 8465 = ☐ + 400 + 60 + 5

3. 3657 = 3000 + ☐ + 50 + 7

4. 7895 = 7000 + 800 + ☐ + 5

5. 6218 = ☐ + 200 + 10 + 8

Write these as numbers.

6. two thousand one hundred and eight ☐

7. four thousand and ninety ☐

8. seven thousand two hundred and thirty-five ☐

9. three thousand eight hundred and sixteen ☐

10. nine thousand seven hundred ☐

Colour in your score

Test 1

Test 2 Addition and subtraction

Knowing **number facts** can help you to work out other calculations.

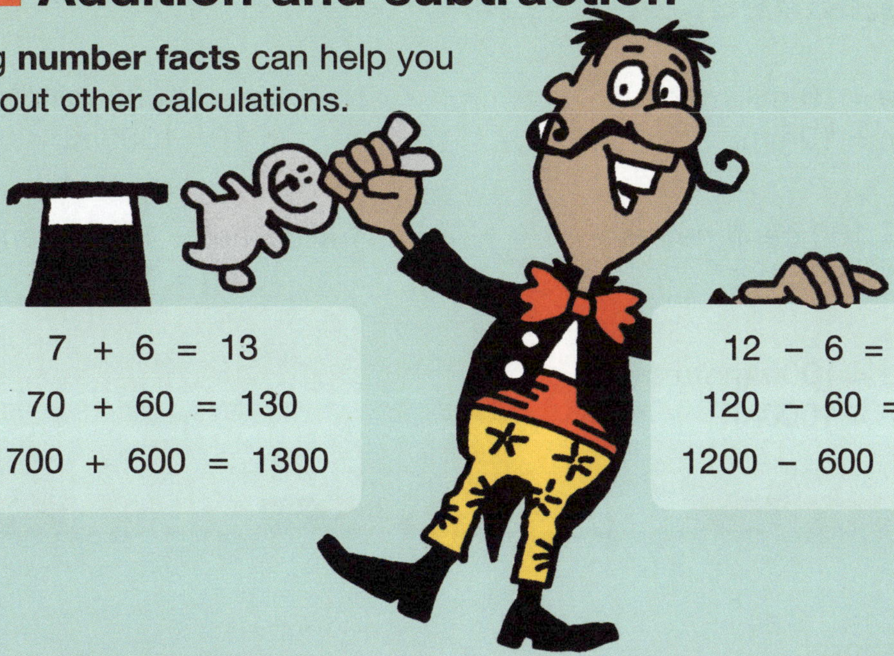

7 + 6 = 13	12 − 6 = 6
70 + 60 = 130	120 − 60 = 60
700 + 600 = 1300	1200 − 600 = 600

Answer these.

1. 40 + 70 =
2. 90 − 30 =
3. 130 − 50 =
4. 600 + 800 =
5. 900 − 400 =
6. 1200 + 500 =
7. 900 + 700 =
8. 170 − 80 =
9. 190 − 120 =
10. 800 + 500 =

10
9
8
7
6
5
4
3
2
1
Colour in your score

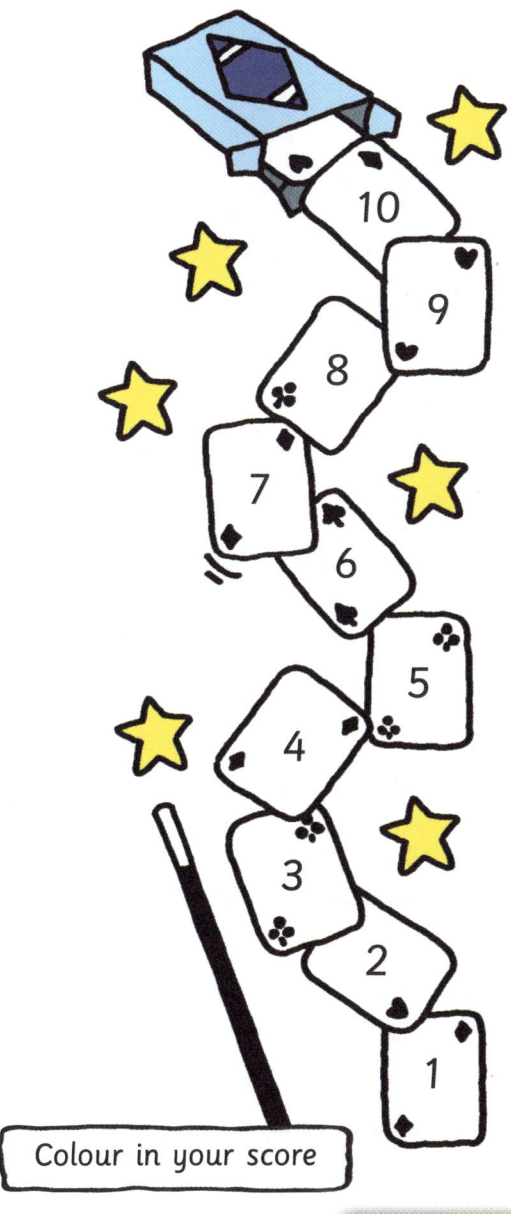

Test 3 Measures

1 centimetre = 10 millimetres 1cm = 10mm	1 litre = 1000 millilitres 1l = 1000ml
1 metre = 100 centimetres 1m = 100cm	1 kilogram = 1000 grams 1kg = 1000g
1 kilometre = 1000 metres 1km = 1000m	

Answer these questions.

1. $\frac{1}{2}$ m = ☐ cm

4. $\frac{1}{4}$ l = ☐ ml

2. $\frac{1}{2}$ cm = ☐ mm

5. $\frac{1}{4}$ kg = ☐ g

3. $\frac{1}{10}$ km = ☐ m

Measure these lines with a ruler.

6. ☐ mm

7.  ☐ mm

8.  ☐ mm

9.  ☐ mm

10.  ☐ mm

Colour in your score

Test 3

Test 4 2D shapes

A **polygon** is any 2D shape with straight sides.

A **regular polygon's** sides and angles are all equal.

How many sides have each of these shapes?

1. A quadrilateral has [ ] sides.

2. An octagon has [ ] sides.

3. A hexagon has [ ] sides.

4. A triangle has [ ] sides.

5. A pentagon has [ ] sides.

Name these shapes.

6. _____

7. _____

8. _____

9. _____

10. _____

Colour in your score

Test 4

Test 5 Number sequences

Number patterns can go up or down.

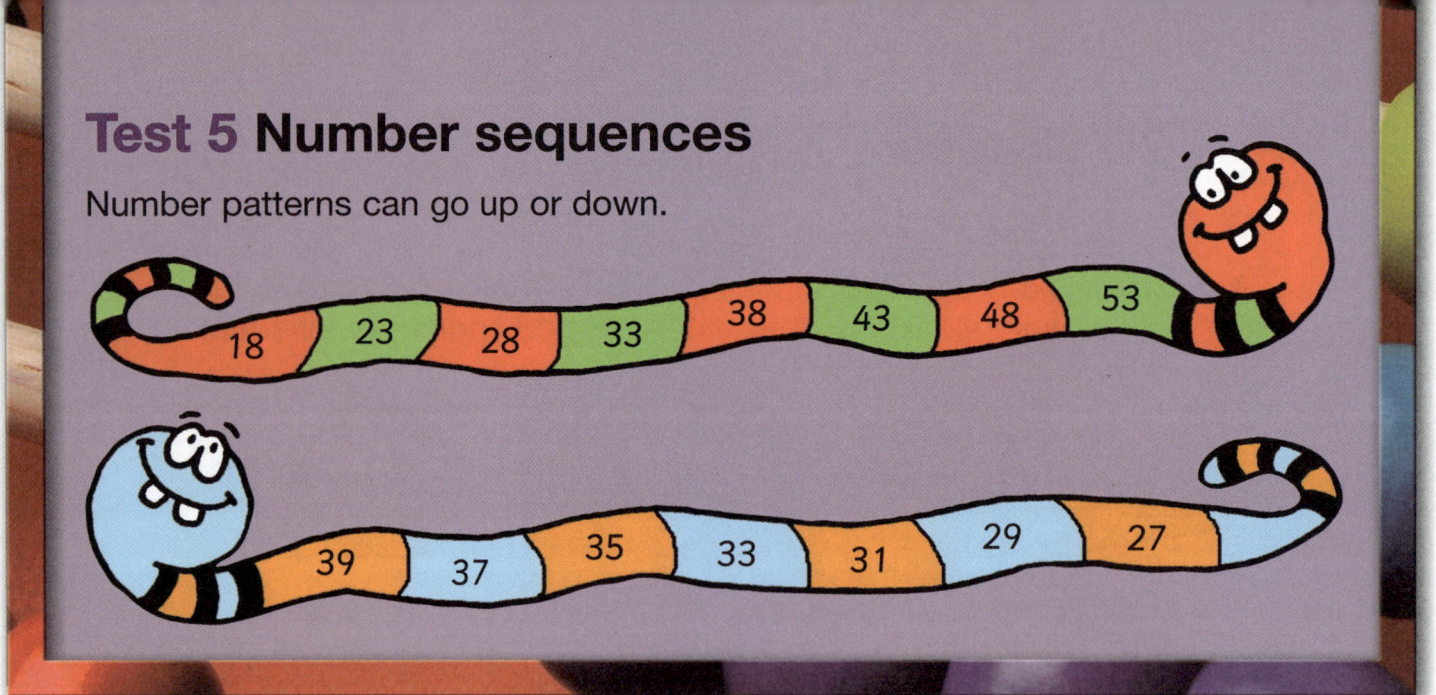

Write the missing numbers in these sequences.

1. 32 | 35 | 38 | ☐ | 44 | 47 | 50 | 53 | ☐ | 59

2. 48 | 52 | ☐ | 60 | 64 | 68 | ☐ | 76 | 80 | 84

3. 31 | 29 | 27 | ☐ | 23 | 21 | ☐ | 17 | 15

4. 230 | 210 | ☐ | 170 | 150 | ☐ | 110 | 90 | 70

5. 76 | 81 | 86 | 91 | ☐ | 101 | 106 | ☐ | 116

Write the missing numbers on these number lines.

6. **7.**

−5 −4 −3 ☐ −1 0 1 2 3 ☐ 5

8. **9.** **10.**

☐ −6 −5 −4 ☐ −2 ☐ 0 1 2 3

Colour in your score

Test 5

Test 6 Multiplication tables

You need to know your **tables**.

Remember, **4 x 6** is the same as **6 x 4**.

It doesn't matter which way round you multiply.

Write the missing numbers.

1. $7 \times \boxed{} = 35$

2. $\boxed{} \times 4 = 40$

3. $8 \times 3 = \boxed{}$

4. $\boxed{} \times 7 = 28$

5. $2 \times \boxed{} = 18$

6. $8 \times \boxed{} = 40$

7. $10 \times 6 = \boxed{}$

8. $\boxed{} \times 3 = 27$

9. $\boxed{} \times 6 = 36$

10. $4 \times \boxed{} = 36$

Colour in your score

Test 6

£1 = 100p

£1.50 = 150p

£0.75 = 75p

£3.25 = 325p

Convert these amounts into pounds or pence.

1. £2.35 = [   ] p

2. £6.45 = [   ] p

3. £ [   ] = 370p

4. £1.09 = [   ] p

5. £ [   ] = 214p

6. £2.75 = [   ] p

Write the totals.

7. £1.85 → 70p → £ [   ]

8. 65p → £2.50 → £ [   ]

9. 90p → £3.15 → £ [   ]

10. £1.90 → £2.20 → £ [   ]

Colour in your score

Test 8 Fractions (1)

Fractions which are the same value are called **equivalent fractions**.

$\frac{2}{4}$ is the same as $\frac{1}{2}$

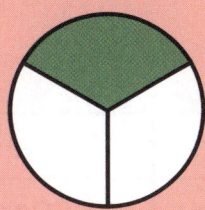 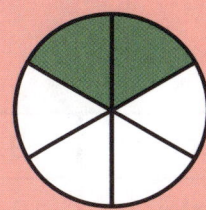

$\frac{1}{3}$ is the same as $\frac{2}{6}$

Write the fractions which are shaded.

1. 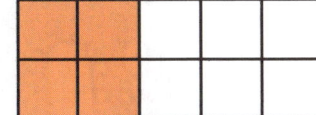　　$\frac{\square}{10} = \frac{\square}{5}$

2. 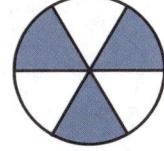　　$\frac{\square}{6} = \frac{\square}{2}$

3. 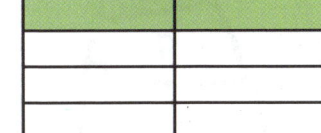　　$\frac{\square}{8} = \frac{\square}{4}$

4. 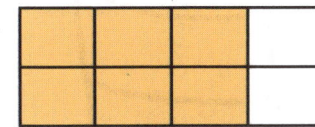　　$\frac{\square}{8} = \frac{\square}{4}$

5. 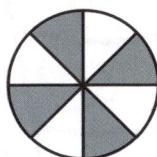　　$\frac{\square}{8} = \frac{\square}{2}$

Complete these fractions.

6. $\frac{4}{5} = \frac{8}{\square}$　　7. $\frac{2}{3} = \frac{\square}{9}$　　8. $\frac{1}{\square} = \frac{3}{12}$

9. $\frac{3}{4} = \frac{\square}{12}$　　10. $\frac{3}{10} = \frac{6}{\square}$

Colour in your score

10
9
8
7
6
5
4
3
2
1

Choc

Choc

Test 8

Test 9 Time

Mornings and **afternoons** are shown by **am** and **pm**.

7.25am ⟶ this is in the morning.

7.25pm ⟶ this is in the evening.

Aston	9.55am	10.45am	11.50am
Banley	10.25am	11.20am	12.25pm
Compton	10.40am	11.40am	12.50pm
Dinsford	11.30am	12.20pm	1.45pm

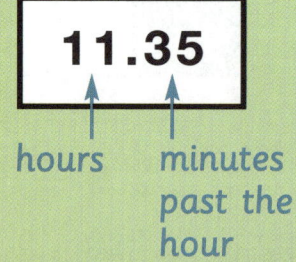

11.35

hours   minutes past the hour

How many minutes do these train journeys take?

1. 9.55am Aston ➡ Banley [ ] minutes

2. 11.20am Banley ➡ Compton [ ] minutes

3. 12.50pm Compton ➡ Dinsford [ ] minutes

4. 10.45am Aston ➡ Compton [ ] minutes

5. 10.25am Banley ➡ Dinsford [ ] minutes

Draw the hands on each clock to show the time.

6. | 8.55 |

7. | 3.45 |

8. | 10.35 |

9. | 12.40 |

10. | 1.05 |

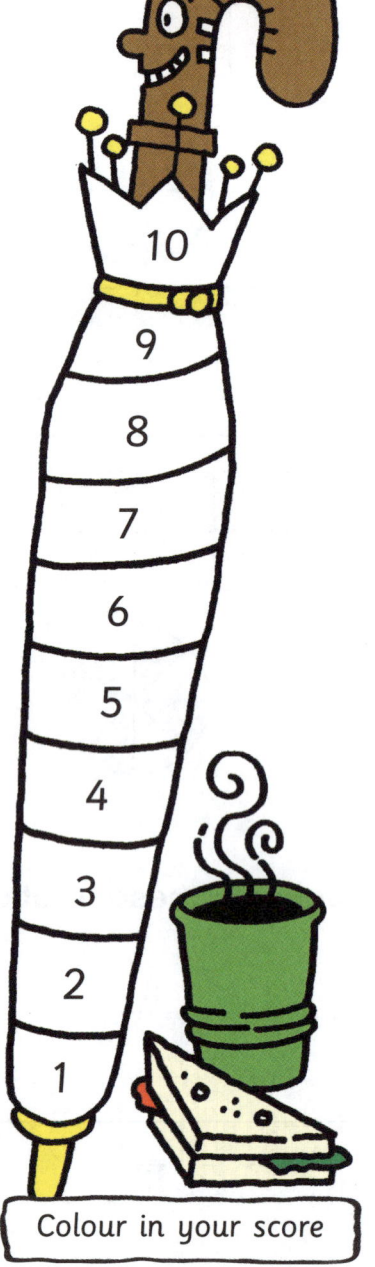

Colour in your score

Test 9

Test 10 Data handling (1)

This **pictogram** shows information about 4 buses that make the same journey at different times.

Bus	Number of people on each bus
A	★ ★ ⯪
B	★ ★
C	★ ★ ★ ★ ★ ⯪
D	★ ★ ★

★ 5 people

⯪ between 1 and 5 people

Passengers on bus C

Adults	Children	Babies

😊😊 = 2 people   😊 = 1 person

1. How many people travelled on bus B? ☐

2. How many people travelled on bus D? ☐

3. Approximately how many people travelled on bus A?

   Between ☐ and ☐

4. Approximately how many people travelled on bus C?

   Between ☐ and ☐

5. Approximately how many people travelled altogether on all 4 buses?

   Between ☐ and ☐

6. How many adults travelled on bus C? ☐

7. How many children travelled on bus C? ☐

8. How many babies travelled on bus C? ☐

9. How many more adults than children travelled on bus C? ☐

10. How many people travelled altogether on bus C? ☐

Colour in your score

Test 10

Test 11 Multiplying and dividing by 10

To **multiply by 10**, move all the digits to the **left**. The empty place is filled by a zero.

$$75 \times 10 =$$
750

To **divide by 10**, move all the digits one place to the **right**.

$$230 \div 10 =$$
23

Multiply each of these numbers by 10.

1. 45   x 10 ⇨ ☐

2. 63   x 10 ⇨ ☐

3. 81   x 10 ⇨ ☐

4. 107   x 10 ⇨ ☐

5. 234   x 10 ⇨ ☐

Divide each of these numbers by 10.

6. 530   ÷10 ⇨ ☐

7. 470   ÷10 ⇨ ☐

8. 380   ÷10 ⇨ ☐

9. 6350   ÷10 ⇨ ☐

10. 8010   ÷10 ⇨ ☐

10
9
8
7
6
5
4
3
2
1

Colour in your score

Test 11

Test 12 Addition

Use mental methods to answer these.

1.   48 + 30 =

2.   36 + 23 =

3.   44 + 46 =

4.   38 + 70 =

5.   56 + 29 =

6.   48 + 37 =

7.   81 + 63 =

8.   72 + 49 =

9.   39 + 45 =

10.   57 + 74 =

Colour in your score

Test 12

Test 13 Money: adding coins

When adding coins, start with the **highest value** coins to make it easier.

Write these totals.

1. £1 20p 20p 50p 2p ⇨ [ ]

2. £1 £1 20p 50p 10p ⇨ [ ]

3. 50p 20p £2 2p 5p ⇨ [ ]

4. 10p 1p 2p £2 £2 ⇨ [ ]

5. 10p 50p 2p 5p £1 ⇨ [ ]

Which coins would you use to buy these books?

6.  £4.90 _____

7. £3.50 _____

8. £1.13 _____

9. £2.26 _____

10. £4.14 _____

Colour in your score

Test 13

Test 14 Measures problems

When doing **measures problems**, make sure you read the questions carefully and then work out what calculations you need to do.

C 192cm

D 240cm

A 135cm

B 155cm

1. What is the difference in length between the longest and shortest ropes?

[ ] cm

2. How much longer is rope C than rope B?

[ ] cm

3. What is the total length of ropes A and B?

[ ] cm

4. Which rope is 85cm longer than rope B?

[ ]

5. Which rope can be cut into 5 equal lengths of 27cm?

[ ]

Work out the answers to these problems.

6. A chef has a 630g bag of flour and uses 85g. How much flour is left in the bag?

[ ] g

7. Alex drove 5800km in one year and 7600km the following year. How much further did he drive in the second year?

[ ] km

8. If 38g of cake mixture is needed to make 1 cake, how much is needed to make 6 cakes?

[ ] g

9. Vikram swam 850m for a sponsored swim. He swam in widths of 10m. How many widths did he swim?

[ ]

10. A pack of 6 cartons has 1260ml of drinks in total. A can holds 240ml. Which holds more, a can or a carton?

[ ]

Colour in your score

Test 14

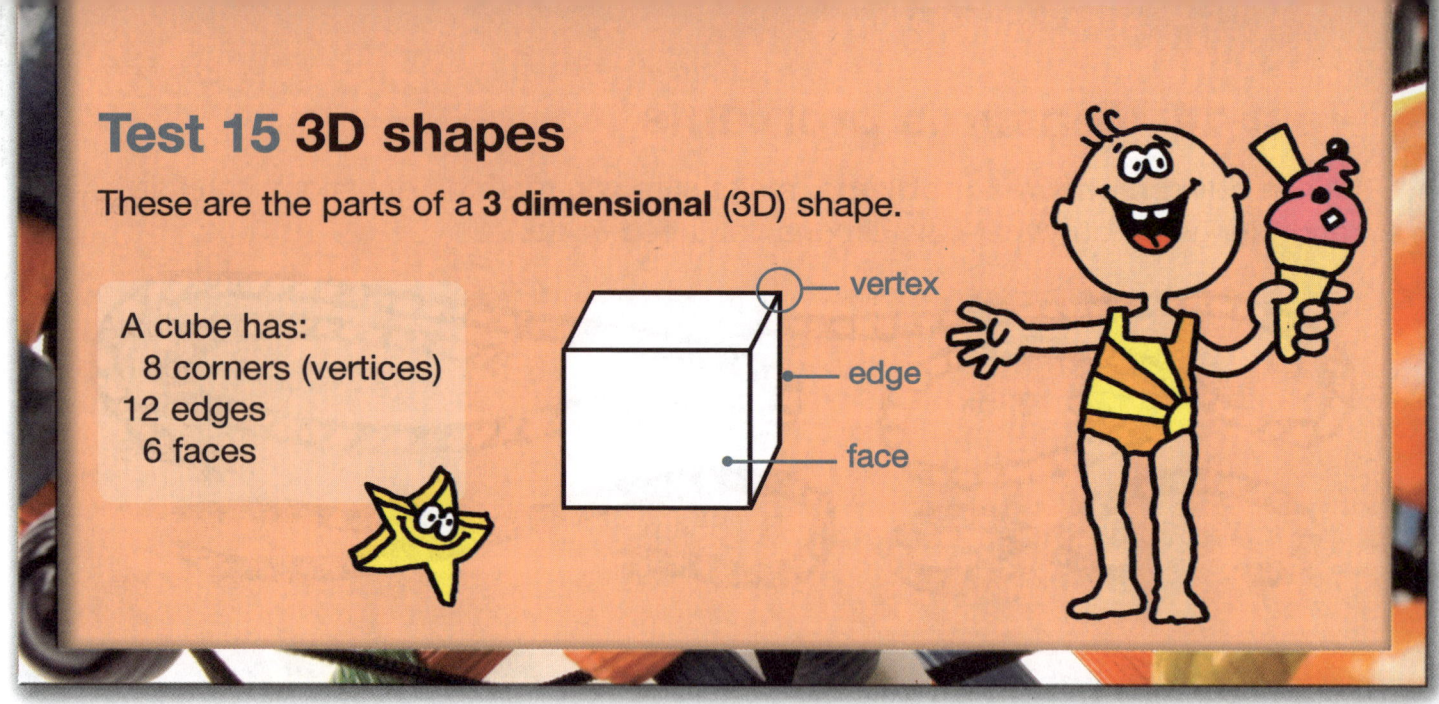

Test 15 **3D shapes**

These are the parts of a **3 dimensional** (3D) shape.

A cube has:
  8 corners (vertices)
  12 edges
  6 faces

vertex
edge
face

Name each shape. Write the missing numbers of corners, edges or faces.

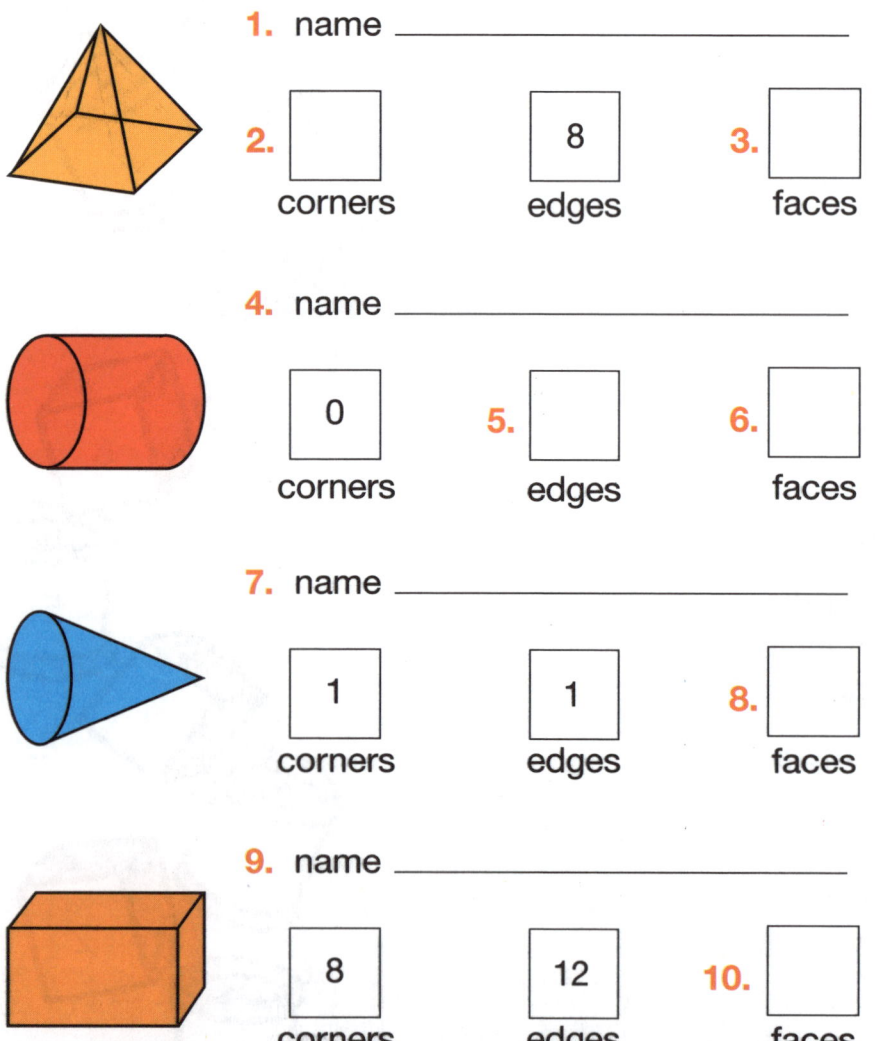

1. name _____

2. [ ] corners   [8] edges   3. [ ] faces

4. name _____

[0] corners   5. [ ] edges   6. [ ] faces

7. name _____

[1] corners   [1] edges   8. [ ] faces

9. name _____

[8] corners   [12] edges   10. [ ] faces

10
9
8
7
6
5
4
3
2
1

Colour in your score

Test 15

Test 16 Number patterns

Look for number patterns.

1	2	3	4	5	6
7	8	9	10	11	12
13	14	15	16	17	18
19	20	21	22	23	24
25	26	27	28	29	30
31	32	33	34	35	36

Write the next number in each number pattern.

1. 12 | 14 | 16 | 18 | 20 | ☐

2. 15 | 18 | 21 | 24 | 27 | ☐

3. 9 | 11 | 13 | 15 | 17 | ☐

4. 33 | 30 | 27 | 24 | 21 | ☐

5. 16 | 20 | 24 | 28 | 32 | ☐

Write the missing number in each number pattern.

6. 22 | 20 | 18 | ☐ | 14 | 12 | 10

7. 27 | 24 | ☐ | 18 | 15 | 12 | 9

8. ☐ | 28 | 30 | 32 | 34 | 36 | 38

9. 36 | 32 | 28 | ☐ | 20 | 16 | 12

10. 9 | 12 | 15 | 18 | ☐ | 24 | 27

Colour in your score

Test 16

Test 17 Division

Use multiplication to help work out **division** questions.

$$24 \div 6 = \boxed{} \Rightarrow 6 \times \boxed{} = 24$$
$$6 \times 4 = 24$$
$$\Downarrow$$
$$24 \div 6 = 4$$

If a number cannot be divided exactly, it leaves a remainder.

$$26 \div 4 = 6 \text{ remainder } 2$$

Answer these.

1. $30 \div 5 = $

2. $32 \div 4 = $

3. $42 \div 3 = $

4. $52 \div 2 = $

5. $85 \div 5 = $

Answer these and write the remainder.

6. $34 \div 4 = $ remainder

7. $29 \div 2 = $ remainder

8. $58 \div 5 = $ remainder

9. $47 \div 3 = $ remainder

10. $86 \div 10 = $ remainder

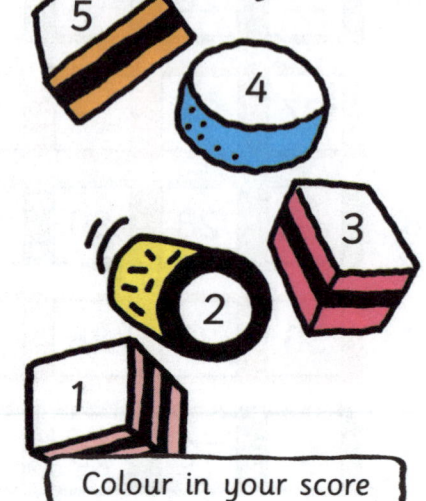

Colour in your score

Test 18 Money problems (1)

When finding the **difference** between two amounts, **count on** from the **lower** amount.

The **difference** between £1.80 and £3.30 is **£1.50** (20p + £1 + 30p).

£1.80   + 20p   + £1   + 30p   £3.30

£2.00   £3.00

Write the difference between these prices.

1. £2.40   £3.50   [ ]

2. £1.70   £2.25   [ ]

3. £2.40   £1.60   [ ]

4. £2.34   £1.50   [ ]

5. £1.95   £1.10   [ ]

6. £3.45   £2.90   [ ]

7. £4.72   £2.80   [ ]

8. £1.30   £4.65   [ ]

9. £2.63   £1.20   [ ]

10. £4.18   £2.80   [ ]

Colour in your score

10 9 8 7 6 5 4 3 2 1

Test 18

Test 19 Fractions (2)

$\frac{1}{3}$ of 15 **is the same as** $15 \div 3 = 5$

Work out the answers.

1. $\frac{1}{4}$ of 12 =

2. $\frac{1}{2}$ of 28 =

3. $\frac{1}{3}$ of 18 =

4. $\frac{1}{5}$ of 20 =

5. $\frac{1}{4}$ of 16 =

6. $\frac{1}{10}$ of 60 =

7. $\frac{1}{3}$ of 24 =

8. $\frac{1}{5}$ of 35 =

9. $\frac{1}{4}$ of 32 =

10. $\frac{1}{10}$ of 90 =

Colour in your score

Test 20 Data handling (2)

The numbers 1-10 have been sorted on these two diagrams.

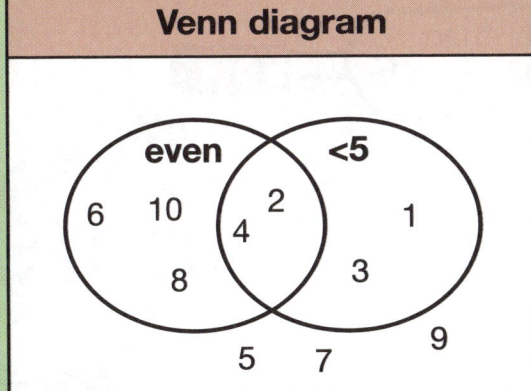

	Venn diagram

Carroll diagram	even	not even
<5	2 4	1 3
not <5	6 10 8	5 9 7

Venn diagram:
even: 6 10 8
overlap: 2 4
<5: 1 3
outside: 5 7 9

Write the numbers in the correct place on each diagram.

> means greater than
< means less than

1. 7

2. 31

3. 28

4. 16

5. 19

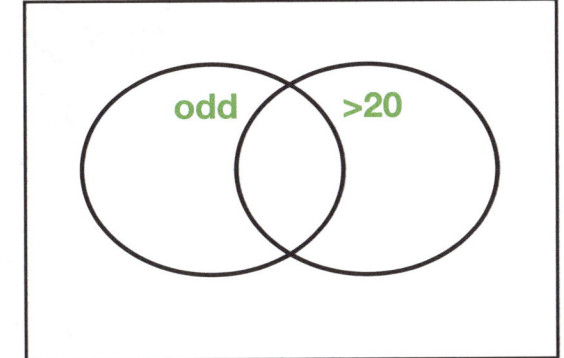

odd   >20

6. 24

7. 13

8. 15

9. 1

10. 6

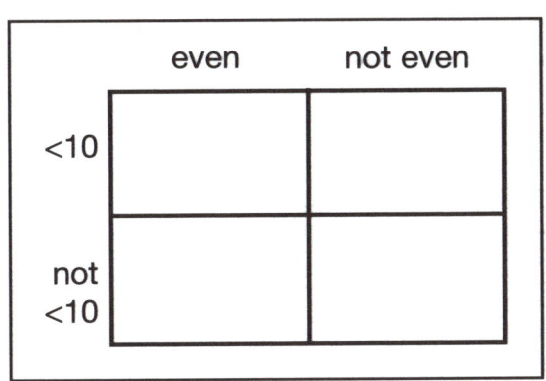

	even	not even
<10		
not <10		

Colour in your score

Test 20

Test 21 Place value (2)

To help work out the **order of numbers**, you can write them in a list, lining up the units columns.

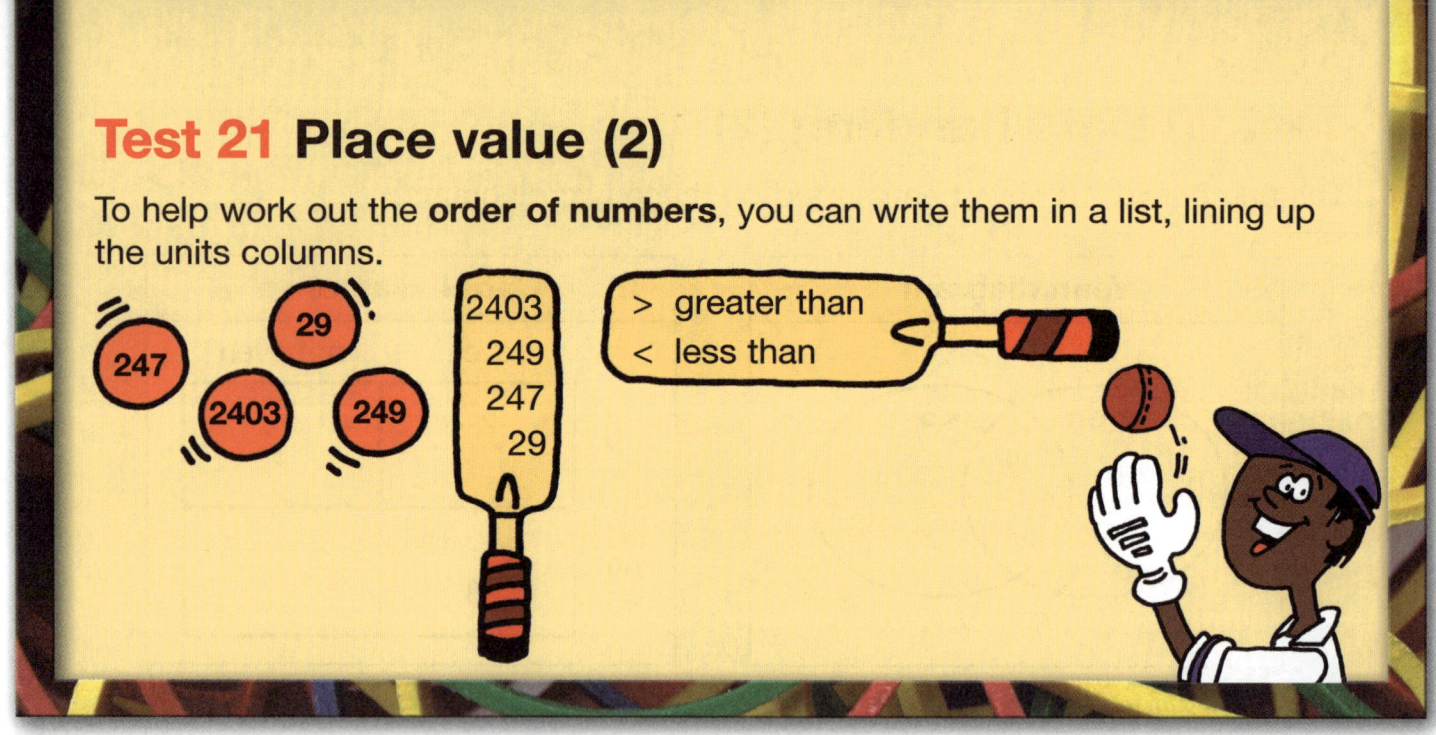

> greater than
< less than

Write the signs > or < for each pair of numbers.

1. 6093 ☐ 6103

2. 4206 ☐ 4311

3. 7415 ☐ 7409

4. 2046 ☐ 2050

5. 8114 ☐ 8108

Write the numbers in order starting with the smallest.

6. 318 308 381 310 ☐ ☐ ☐ ☐

7. 4081 4180 4191 4008 ☐ ☐ ☐ ☐

8. 6095 6293 6120 6905 ☐ ☐ ☐ ☐

9. 2140 2004 410 4010 ☐ ☐ ☐ ☐

10. 9214 902 9189 989 ☐ ☐ ☐ ☐

Colour in your score

Test 22 Subtraction

There are lots of ways to **take one number from another**. Look at the numbers carefully and work out the best mental method to use for those numbers.

Use mental methods to answer these.

1.   42   –   29   =   [   ]

2.   57   –   23   =   [   ]

3.   31   –   17   =   [   ]

4.   62   –   31   =   [   ]

5.   54   –   19   =   [   ]

6.   81   –   4   =   [   ]

7.   305 –   9   =   [   ]

8.   63   –   38   =   [   ]

9.   52   –   7   =   [   ]

10. 89   –   35   =   [   ]

10
9
8
7
6
5
4
3
2
1

Colour in your score

Test 22

Test 23 Area

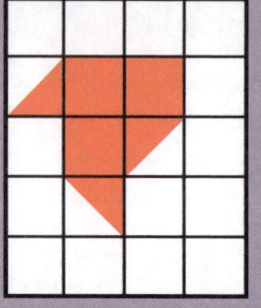 

To work out the area of an **irregular shape**, count the whole squares.

$\frac{1}{2}$ or more squares count as whole squares.

Ignore squares less than $\frac{1}{2}$.

For shapes with **straight sides**, count $\frac{1}{2}$ squares.

Work out the areas of these shapes.

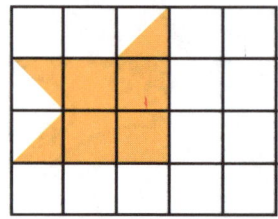 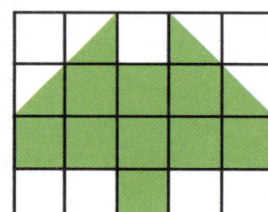 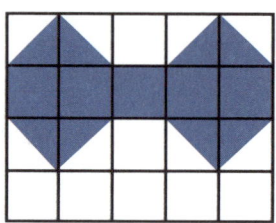

1. ☐ squares   2. ☐ squares   3. ☐ squares

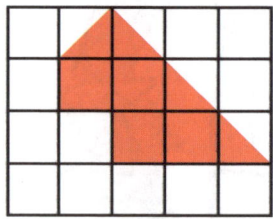  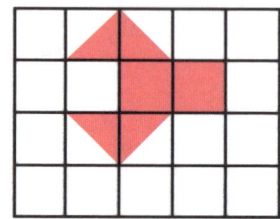

4. ☐ squares   5. ☐ squares   6. ☐ squares

Work out the approximate areas of these shapes.

7.   8.   9.   10.

   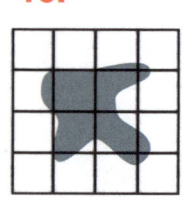

☐ squares   ☐ squares   ☐ squares   ☐ squares

10
9
8
7
6
5
4
3
2
1

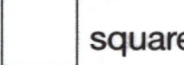 Colour in your score

Test 23

Test 24 Shape: symmetry

A shape has line **symmetry** if both sides are exactly the same when a mirror line is drawn.

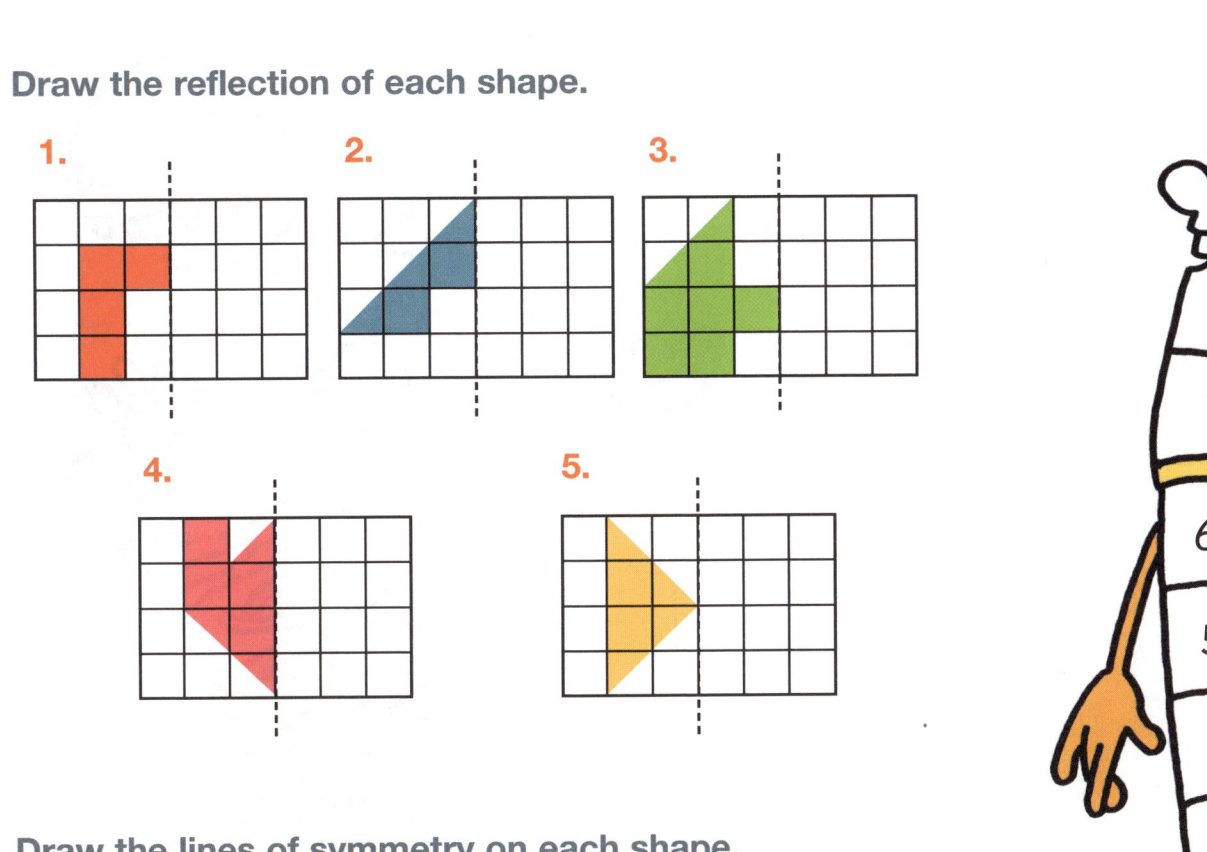

A shape reflected in a mirror.   1 line of symmetry.   2 lines of symmetry.

Draw the reflection of each shape.

1.

2.

3.

4.

5.

Draw the lines of symmetry on each shape.

6.

7.

8.

9.

10.

Colour in your score

Test 24

Test 25 Multiples

Multiples of 2 are: 2, 4, 6, 8, 10, 12... and so on.

Multiples of 3 are: 3, 6, 9, 12, 15, 18... and so on.

Multiples of a number do not come to an end at x10, they go on and on. So, for example, 82, 94, 106 and 300 are all multiples of 2.

Which of these numbers are multiples of 2, 3, 4 or 5? Some numbers are used more than once.

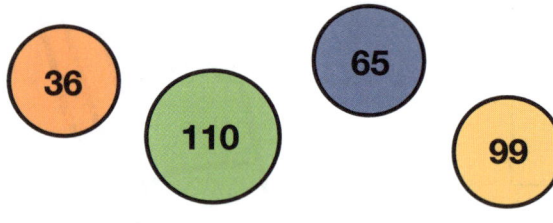

36   110   65   99   92   111

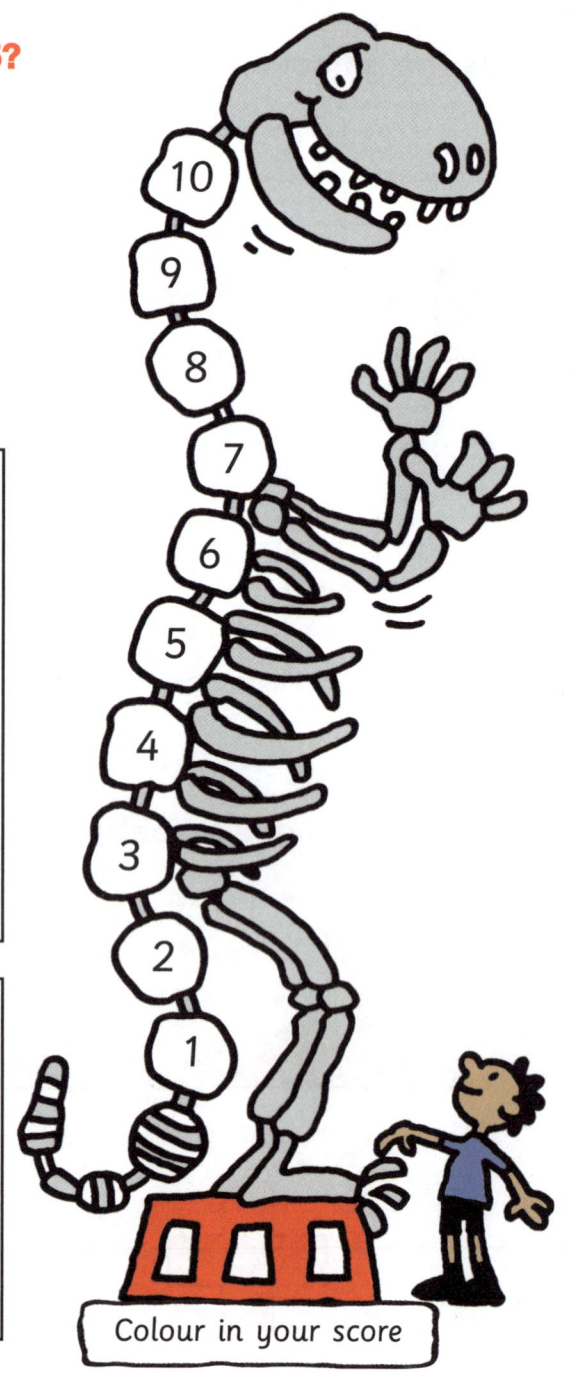

Multiples of 2

1.
2.
3.

Multiples of 3

4.
5.
6.

Multiples of 4

7.
8.

Multiples of 5

9.
10.

Colour in your score

Test 25

Test 26 Multiplication

When **multiplying** it can help to break numbers up.

$43 \times 5 =$

40×5	$=$	200
3×5	$=$	$+ \ 15$
43×5	$=$	215

$$\begin{array}{r} 4\ 3 \\ \times \quad 5 \\ \hline 2\ 1\ 5 \\ \hline 1 \end{array}$$

Answer these.

1. $36 \times 3 =$

2. $41 \times 4 =$

3. $53 \times 2 =$

4. $47 \times 3 =$

5. $56 \times 4 =$

Answer these.

6.
$$\begin{array}{r} 5\ 3 \\ \times \quad 3 \\ \hline \end{array}$$

7.
$$\begin{array}{r} 8\ 4 \\ \times \quad 2 \\ \hline \end{array}$$

8.
$$\begin{array}{r} 6\ 7 \\ \times \quad 4 \\ \hline \end{array}$$

9.
$$\begin{array}{r} 7\ 4 \\ \times \quad 3 \\ \hline \end{array}$$

10.
$$\begin{array}{r} 5\ 9 \\ \times \quad 5 \\ \hline \end{array}$$

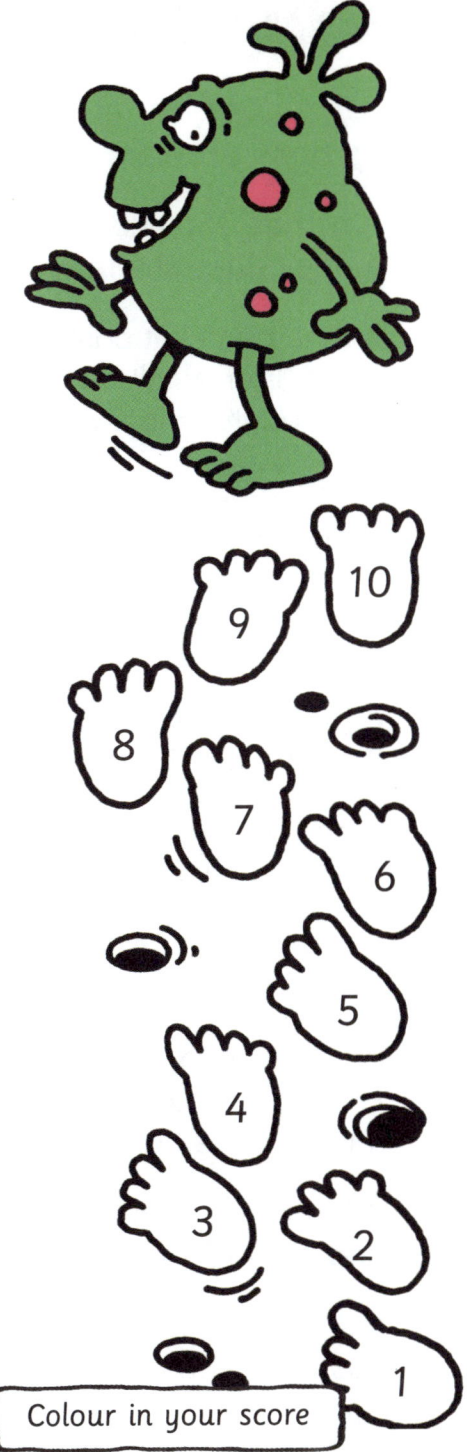

Colour in your score

Test 26

Test 27 Money problems (2)

When working out **word problems**, read the questions carefully to work out the calculations you need to do.

Answer these problems.

1. Amy has 95p and spends 57p. How much money does she have left?

2. A cinema ticket costs £3.50 for an adult and £3 for a child. What is the total cost for 2 adults and 2 children?

3. A newspaper costs 35p. What is the cost for a week's supply of newspapers?

4. A sweet costs 14p. How many can be bought for £1?

5. A bus journey costs £1.20. How much will the total fare be for 4 people?

6. A car costs £2400. If it is reduced by £800, how much will it cost?

7. A book costs £4.70. It is reduced by £1.90 in a sale. What is the new price of the book?

8. Sam has two 20p coins and a 50p coin. He buys a magazine at 72p. How much money does he have left?

9. What is the total cost of a £4.50 T-shirt and a £3.70 pair of shorts?

10. If a fairground ride costs 80p, what is the cost of 3 rides?

Colour in your score

Test 27

Test 28 Decimals

A **decimal point** is used to separate whole numbers from fractions.

$0.1 = \frac{1}{10}$ $0.2 = \frac{2}{10}$ $0.5 = \frac{1}{2}$

tens	units		tenths
8	2	·	6
80	2		$\frac{6}{10}$

Change these fractions to decimals.

1. $\frac{7}{10}$ = ☐

2. $1\frac{1}{2}$ = ☐

3. $3\frac{3}{10}$ = ☐

4. $\frac{9}{10}$ = ☐

5. $2\frac{4}{10}$ = ☐

Write the decimals on this number line.

6. ☐   7. ☐   8. ☐   9. ☐   10. ☐

0 ├─┼─┼─┼─┼─┼─┼─┼─┼─┼─┤ 1

Colour in your score

Test 28

The same time can look different.

These clocks are 45 minutes fast.
Write the real time for each of them.

1.

4.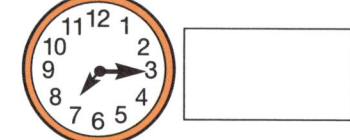

2.

5.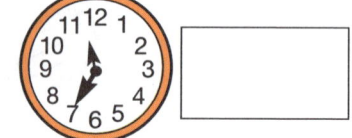

3.

A train takes 20 minutes between each of these stations.
Complete the timetable.

6.	Smedley	2.10	
7.	Chadwick		4.45
8.	Welby	2.50	
9.	Burnsford		5.25
10.	Ragby		5.45

10
9
8
7
6
5
4
3
2
1

Colour in your score

Test 30 Data handling (3)

These **graphs** show the number of cans collected by two classes in a school over a month.

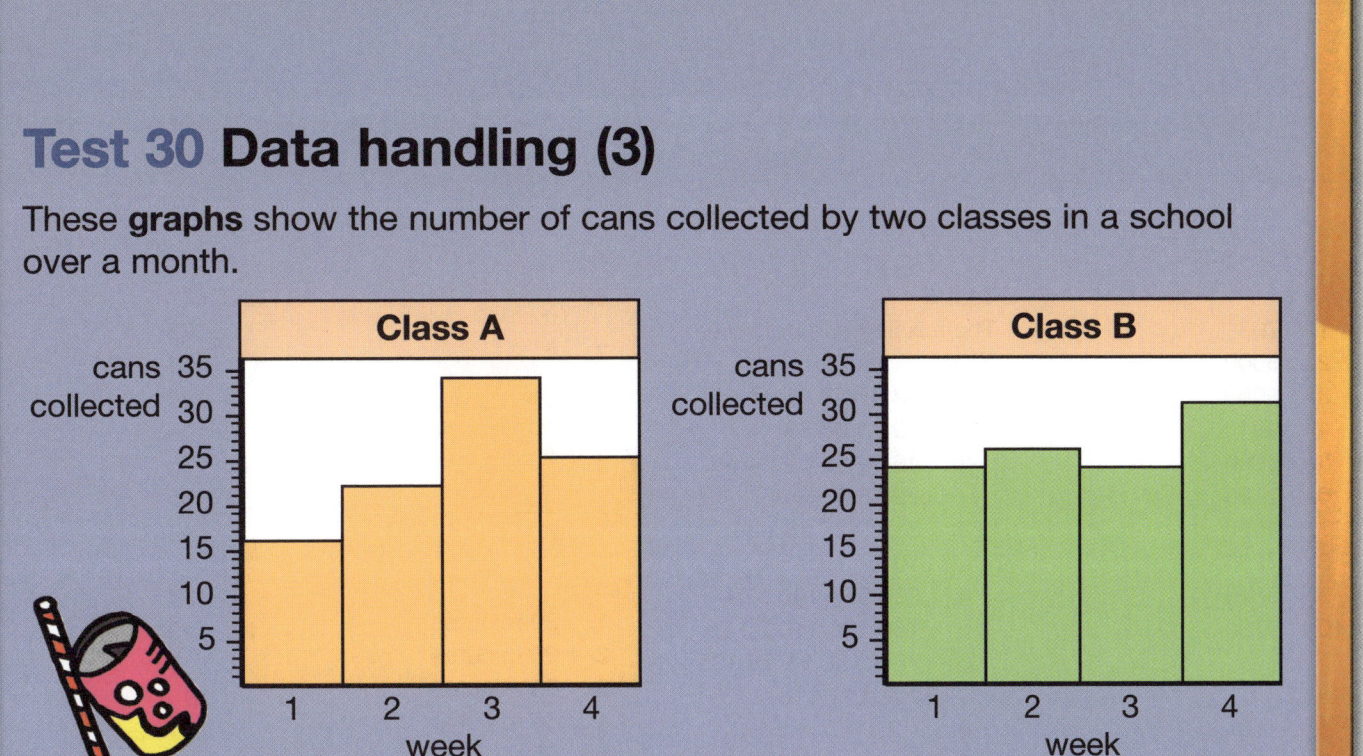

Answer these problems.

1. How many cans were collected by Class A in week 2?

2. How many cans were collected by Class B in week 1?

3. In which week did Class A collect 25 cans?

4. How many more cans were collected in week 1 by Class B than by Class A?

5. In which week did Class A collect 10 more cans than Class B?

6. In which week did Class B collect 26 cans?

7. In which 2 weeks were the same number of cans collected by Class B?

8. How many more cans were collected in week 3 by Class A than by Class B?

9. How many cans altogether were collected by Class B?

10. Which class collected the most cans?

Colour in your score

Test 30

ANSWERS

Test 1
1. 70
2. 8000
3. 600
4. 90
5. 6000
6. 2108
7. 4090
8. 7235
9. 3816
10. 9700

Test 2
1. 110
2. 60
3. 80
4. 1400
5. 500
6. 1700
7. 1600
8. 90
9. 70
10. 1300

Test 3
1. 50cm
2. 5mm
3. 100m
4. 250ml
5. 250g
6. 38mm
7. 52mm
8. 63mm
9. 26mm
10. 77mm

Test 4
1. 4
2. 8
3. 6
4. 3
5. 5
6. pentagon
7. hexagon
8. octagon
9. quadrilateral
10. triangle

Test 5
The missing numbers are in **bold**.
1. 32 35 38 **41** 44 47 50 53 **56** 59
2. 48 52 **56** 60 64 68 **72** 76 80 84
3. 31 29 27 **25** 23 21 **19** 17 15
4. 230 210 **190** 170 150 **130** 110 90 70
5. 76 81 86 91 **96** 101 106 **111** 116
6. – 2
7. 4
8. – 7
9. – 3
10. – 1

Test 6
1. 5
2. 10
3. 24
4. 4
5. 9
6. 5
7. 60
8. 9
9. 6
10. 9

Test 7
1. 235p
2. 645p
3. £3.70
4. 109p
5. £2.14
6. 275p
7. £2.55
8. £3.15
9. £4.05
10. £4.10

Test 8
1. $\frac{4}{10}$ = $\frac{2}{5}$
2. $\frac{3}{6}$ = $\frac{1}{2}$
3. $\frac{2}{8}$ = $\frac{1}{4}$
4. $\frac{6}{8}$ = $\frac{3}{4}$
5. $\frac{4}{8}$ = $\frac{1}{2}$
6. $\frac{8}{10}$
7. $\frac{6}{9}$
8. $\frac{1}{4}$
9. $\frac{9}{12}$
10. $\frac{6}{20}$

Test 9
1. 30 minutes
2. 20 minutes
3. 55 minutes
4. 55 minutes
5. 65 minutes
6.
7.
8.
9.
10.

Test 10
1. 10
2. 15
3. Between 11 and 15.
4. Between 26 and 30.
5. Between 62 and 70.
6. 14
7. 9
8. 5
9. 5
10. 28

Test 11
1. 450
2. 630
3. 810
4. 1070
5. 2340
6. 53
7. 47
8. 38
9. 635
10. 801

Test 12
1. 78
2. 59
3. 90
4. 108
5. 85
6. 85
7. 144
8. 121
9. 84
10. 131

Test 13
1. £1.92
2. £2.80
3. £2.77
4. £4.13
5. £1.67
6. £2 £2 50p 20p 20p
7. £2 £1 50p
8. £1 10p 2p 1p
9. £2 20p 5p 1p
10. £2 £2 10p 2p 2p

Test 14
1. 105cm
2. 37cm
3. 290cm
4. D
5. A
6. 545g
7. 1800km
8. 228g
9. 85
10. can

Test 15
1. pyramid
2. 5 corners
3. 5 faces
4. cylinder
5. 2 edges
6. 3 faces
7. cone
8. 2 faces
9. cuboid
10. 6 faces